Gather up the Fragments

The poetry of Shelby Scott

www.TotalPublishingAndMedia.com

Gather up the Fragments

ISBN: 978-1-63302-055-9

Copyright 2016 by Shelby Scott

Published by Total Publishing and Media

5411 South 125th East Ave.

Suite 302

Tulsa, OK 74146

www.totalpublishingmedia.com

Printed in the United States of America. All rights reserved under International Copyright Law. Cover and /or contents may not be reproduced in any form without the express written consent of the author.

Acknowledgements

I wish to thank the community of Saint Patrick's for gracious loving; Dr. James Ronda for encouragement and guidance; Dr. Charles Chapman for teaching me the power of a word fitly spoken and sung; and Becky Scott, for fostering vulnerability and manifesting courage.

Contents

Acknowledgements iii

Foreword ix

Gather up the Fragments 15

Ash Wednesday 17

Emptying? 19

Performs what it declares 21

Waiting 23

Snow Cancellations 25

Sabbath 28

"Chaplain for non-contact visit" 30

Not quite yet 33

The Transit of Venus 35

Mary's funeral 36

Political Process Upside Down 38

Long Leg 40

Waiting on Henri Ross 44

Lament	46
Artifact	49
It is summer	53
Opening Day	54
Late Summer Tomatoes	56
Sunflower	59
Grandfather Spindler	62
Black Shoes	63
Bull Trout	67
Where did Summer Go?	70
CA-35	72
Release	74

Baccalaureate
    Prelude in E Flat 76

Tiananmen Square	77
Marlinspike	79
Poem Depression	82
Dental X-rays	84

November Tear 86

Night Terrors 87

Winter Wind 88

The Grand Floridian Hotel 89

Post-election 91

Old Truck 94

Canine Cologne 97

Contentment 99

Cocoon 101

Liminal 103

Vesper Light 104

Shower 106

Samuel 108

About the Author… 111

Weighing Anchor

Shelby Scott – Poet, Priest, and Sailor

We live in a swirl of experience. We are surrounded by happenings, accidents, confusions, and the occasional defining moment. It all happens at once. The needle spins around the compass rose and it's easy for us to lose any sense of direction. What we make of that swirl is in some mysterious way a measure of our lives. We can ignore life's bright mornings and stormy nights. We can hurry through our days with eyes closed, minds already made up, and imaginations permanently fixed on hold. We might even claim citizenship in the United States of Amnesia. Doing that does not mean God loves us any less. What it does mean is that we miss all the wonder and weirdness that surrounds us in creation. We miss out on the silly and the serene, the moments of pain and pure delight.

What you will find revealed in these pages is the result of another set of choices – choices about being open to all the twists and turns, the changes and chances of life at flood tide. Shelby Scott is a poet, a priest, and a sailor. Each of those life pursuits is its own special calling. These are life choices that on any day can be dangerous, rewarding, infuriating, or just plain boring. Each offers much and demands much. Each informs and enriches the other.

Shelby is a poet. Poets don't always write in rhymes. Or, at least they are not required to do that. They do not write jingles but there is always music in every line. Poets take the full range of human experience and then cut to the heart of every moment. Poets do the hard work of selection and compression. They select fragments of life and then compress them into powerful, compelling, memorable words and images. Poets are engaged in revelation. What they reveal is not always what we expect or hope or desire to be made known. Poets are driven to uncover what is so often concealed. They give shape to what is hidden in plain sight. Poetry expands the mind. It enlarges the imagination. It sharpens our vision. It moves us from mere looking to deep seeing; from just hearing to concentrated, intentional listening. Poetry is an exercise in finding meaning in even the most ordinary, the most commonplace moment. Poetry reaches deep and ranges wide. Shelby Scott's poetry takes the swirl of life, sorts it out, compresses it, and then reveals it to be extraordinary, marvelous, and on occasion searingly painful.

Shelby is a priest. It is important to say that these poems make manifest the life of a priest. Shelby's priestly life is woven into the very fabric of his poems. It is equally important to say that these "priestly poems" are not of the "gentle Jesus, meek and mild" variety. Be warned – there is struggle, doubt, and suffering here. George Herbert and John Donne would have understood that. Emily Dickinson and Walt Whitman knew that. Their poetry ventures into some of the darkest chambers of the human heart. Father Shelby knows about some of those dark places. His poems acknowledge the presence of darkness. They seek – even for a moment – to cast some light in the midst of darkness. There is devotion and integrity written across these pages. There are also compelling moments of weakness and failure. All of that is honestly revealed and openly confessed. These poems are deeply personal – sometimes autobiographical – without being obsessively self-referential. In recent times a good deal of poetry has been of the "all me all the time" variety. That is not what you will find here. These poems balance genuine pride of accomplishment with authentic humility. The presence of the divine is infused in these poems. The imprint of a faithful life is set deep in the shape of each word and thought. That presence has molded these poems as it has shaped Father Shelby's life.

Shelby Scott is a sailor. For reasons almost beyond understanding, many young folks growing on the Oklahoma Great Plains are captured by dreams of sailing the boundless seas. Someone once said that doodles in the margins of schoolbooks from the Dakotas to west Texas are sure to be palm trees and sailboats. Born in Duncan, Oklahoma, Shelby Scott was one of those kids seized by the lure of the sea. His poetry is filled with maritime, nautical lingo. There is a lot of sailor talk here. Whether it is salty or not is for you to judge. Shelby's poetry sounds the depths, keeps a weather eye, and pays heed to the tides and currents. His poems tack in the wind; they trace the ebb and flow of his life and ours.

In the safe harbor of a well-deserved sabbatical Shelby Scott gathered entries from the captain's log of his poetry. He once imagined that the sabbatical would be an outward-bound voyage. Instead, he has followed the course set by Henry David Thoreau. In his classic book <u>Walden</u>, Thoreau urges us to make interior voyages, voyages of self-discovery. Shelby Scott has made that inner passage, that journey into the very heart of things. His poems are not merely reports from one personal voyage. They also ask us to make what Lewis and Clark famously called their "tour of discovery." Shelby calls us to look sharp, pay attention, and listen to the wind. Open the book, weigh anchor, and set sail. You are in good and honest hands. These are hands that know the ropes and will help you steer a true course.

James P. Ronda

Gather up the Fragments

He told the disciples to "gather up the fragments"

> they collected twelve baskets full of left over miracle.

Torn chunks of bread. Not multigrain loaves like they sell at Panera,

> but crumbs and portions....

Nothing that you would take to your friend's house to be served at a dinner,

> but broken pieces....

Bread enough to sustain and share,

> not pretty enough to display on the table.
>
>> I guess Jesus didn't want it to develop into pride and competition.

Maybe fragments and pieces are all we really need....

> A few moments of quiet in the rocker by the fireplace
>
>> while I scratch Monte's ears.

A few hours at the lake checking on the boat,

    which whets my appetite for a long sail….

A small intimate Wednesday night Eucharist,

    a foretaste of the heavenly banquet to come.

        The good night kiss and holding your hand is also enough to feed.

November 17, 2014

Ash Wednesday

"You are dust and to dust you shall return."

Repeated each time as I sign the foreheads of

> parishioners, the dust of burnt palms smudging a cross on each presented forehead....

The black dust doesn't just stay put on the forehead,

> it falls,
>
>> sometimes trickles down the cheek
>>
>>> sometimes catching on an eyelash.
>>
>> A little bit of ash falls onto my prayer book
>>
>>> and slides into the crevice between pages 266 and 267....

Maybe that is the goal and end of Lent, a little bit of the darkness gently rubbed away by prayer,

> worn down by time,
>
>> or washed away by a tear....

A winter chill makes it a brisk walk down the sidewalk

    after the early morning service,

        the bluebird perched on the leafless tree,

            awaiting sunlight to make its feathers resplendent.

But this morning,

    this season we still have to endure the gray,

        we have to wait through more mute sunless mornings.

But spring will come,

    as surely as Easter follows these forty days.

                Ash Wednesday, February 13, 2013

Emptying?

Escaping the business of the office

    I slip into the nave.

        A refuge of silence.

The quiet and the hush in the room freshens my soul

    and slows my breathing.

A bearing on the AC unit screeches when the unit kicks on, shattering the peace.

        My mind wanders to the schematics of the unit

            and analyzes what would need to be oiled or replaced.

I try to quiet my mind,

    and allow sounds just to flow through,

        without holding onto the intruding tones.

The advancing afternoon sun shoots a shaft of autumn light

in which dust motes float, rise and drift out of visibility.

Emptying the distractions from my mind seems futile.

    The ringing in my ears demands to be acknowledged,

        self-diagnosis declares it as tinnitus.

            Even the subtle whoosh of blood flowing through my head crosses the threshold of perception and seems audible.

Distractions are always there, flitting in and out of perception.

    Meditation doesn't empty the intrusions from my awareness.

    I leave more attuned to the barrage.

        All Saints, November 3, 2014

Performs what it declares

It is a matter of point of view.

The congregation stares as I lift the chalice,

> slightly bowed heads reverencing.

> Even the most jaded are made a little curious

>> with the stunning declaration, "Holy gifts, for God's Holy people."

They stare at beautiful ordinary things set apart for holy work, linen cloth, silver chalice, and stone altar.

I, however, have an equally stunning point of view.

> I too stare at beautiful things which convey the holy.

>> A husband casually touching the top of his wife's hand during the consecration.

>> A mother emphasizing the Lord's Prayer

>>> to her impressionable young daughter.

Sunlight cascading through windows,

    illuminating faces,

        some with eyes closed while praying fervently.

It is when I lift the chalice

    that I am graced to see the reflection of the cross

        hanging on the wall behind my back.

        The wine a glorious medium,

            transformed by the curvature of the
            chalice and the uplifted reflective cup.

How ironic,

    they think they are staring at what is holy

but I believe

    it is their authentic offering of life, love,

        and hoped- for prayer which is most sacred.

                July 31, 2012

Waiting

His blood pressure is stable, but it feels …different.

    We wait, wondering if we should call our brother in Alabama, or the sister in Florida.

        They have to work and can't be out here waiting at the hospital.

            Dad made it through the hip surgery fine,

                but the pneumonia seems to have gotten more serious.

                Dad also said, "I don't want to do this anymore.
                    I'm tired."

So we wait by his bed,

    watching the bp display as his chest slowly lifts with each shallow breath.

        Should we call? And what would we say?….

        Nothing has medically changed.

Being the younger brother you will ask me if you should come,

> and I don't want the burden to decide for you....

What I want to say is, "Yes!"

> You should be here, not to do anything, but to be.
>
> To bear witness to this great transition....
>
> > I need you to drink bad coffee in Styrofoam cups with me
> >
> > > and to tell the stories of how we acted out when we were kids.
> > >
> > > > But you say your boss needs quarterly reports and to call again when something happens.

June 16, 2015

Snow Cancellations

The meteorologist interrupts the usual programming
warning of snow and possible ice.

> Schools are already closing for the next day in
> anticipation.

>> Snow does come, but not more than two
>> or three inches....

Yes, for Oklahoma it is an "event,"

> and most of the churches cancel Wednesday night
> services.

>> My colleague in a nearby parish says she
>> doesn't want old ladies to fall

>>> (which would cause her to be too
>>> busy with hospital visits).

We don't cancel Evensong; it is not about comfort,
ease, or the challenge of trudging through snow-
covered parking lots..

> It is about God....

sanctifying time, paying respect to the
One who gave us snow,

life, and the privilege to worship….

The dozen or so who journeyed through the weather

did find a warm nave, soft candles

and a beautifully played improvisation on
Wondrous Love.

The organ's Gedekt and flutes toss the
thin melody through the quiet hushed
nave….

Time is set apart, made Holy.

March 5, 2015

Sabbath

I drive more slowly on Fridays,

    my scheduled Sabbath day of rest.

        Cars behind me are annoyed that I mosey along.

How many times have I driven down Wagoner's Main Street and not noticed the Virginia Creeper

    climbing up the side of the red brick building,

        the one next to the Bail Bondsman sign.

Chevy and Ford trucks dusted in red dirt angle park at the café.

    The Antique store and the Tanning Salon are locked up, "out of business" signs taped to the door.

Sitting at the light I feel the weight of economic downturn on Main Street.

    Cars honk,

        startling me,

the light has changed. I give a furtive
apologetic wave.

That is me on other days of the week.

Impatient, rushed, handcuffed to doing.

But today I am created, commanded to observe,

not to do, but be.

It is Sabbath.

Friday, May 30, 2014

"Chaplain for non-contact visit"

Concrete, metal, thick safety glass, define it as "non-contact"….

> The video monitoring and squawky intercom
>> allow no privacy.

Jails are built so nothing can be damaged,
> even the covers for the electrical outlets are secure.

Aesthetics and humanity have no currency when designing a jail.
> Weak plastic chairs misaligned before each cubicle's glass.

The building hums with the sound of a thousand inmates yelling, marking turf, doing time.

The guard shackles his wrist to the wall
> to keep him even more secure in the four foot by seven foot chamber.

Only fourteen years old, yet he is adopting the talk and demeanor of one who is going to do serious time.

His flat affect and mumble makes it really hard to hear.

    I ask perfunctory questions…. "fine," "ok," "getting by"….

        The only place his eyes flicker

            is when I ask about his health.

                "I have gained thirty pounds inside this year, I weigh one forty"….

The visitor behind me starts yelling obscenities

    while this boy-man mumbles

        "There are some really messed up guys in here."….

Oh, I used to teach tenderfoot scouts your age,

    to hike and start a fire….

        to be prepared for any situation….

            but not for this place.

I feel impotent saying a prayer

    in this sterile dark cave.

        Yet, my hand goes to the glass and your hand
           awkwardly reaches ….

Will my prayers fly to heaven?

    Do the concrete ceiling and metal bars block
       their reception as effectively

        as the glass blocks our grasp?

                January 3, 2014

Not quite yet….

The daffodils were a surprise;

I hadn't noticed them growing in the memorial garden,

    near where we had interred Jodie's cremains.

The warm weather coaxed them to show up early….

    though it is only February their brave little yellow faces stood in contrast to the accumulated

        winter detritus.

A harbinger of spring.

    A foretaste of warmer times, the lake, late evenings with the sun still up….

But before I get too excited,

    the forecast calls for snow….

        and reluctantly I have to admit

            the weathermen on Channel 2 are right.

Sleet and wet snow cover the ground,

    the harsh winter wind wraps snow

around the daffodil's shoulders, entombing them.

> They too must wait for the warmth of resurrection.

February 20, 2013

The Transit of Venus

Don't miss it this evening;
    it will not occur for another 145 years.
        When we speak of planets and stars aligning,
            this is what we mean.
What momentous event will occur?
    A president born or second coming?
        The governor of Wisconsin might be recalled….
For several hours Venus will march across the sun,
    a smaller black orb blocking the harsh light,
        which you can only see with filters
            or you might damage your vision….
But I have a meeting,
    and after that, laundry to fold,
        and a call to return….
My vision already damaged by tomorrow's chores….

                                            June 6, 2012

Mary's funeral

The rusted sign in the church parking lot

    reveals the number of Sunday services has decreased over the years.

        Worn off varnish allowed the oak front doors to turn gray streaking where storms

            had taken its toll.

The church was packed.

    A town's respect for Mary.

        For 31 years she had been the church secretary and de facto pastor.

            The decline of the congregation evidenced by the old bulletins piled in a corner

                and the broken chairs stacked in the choir loft

                    awaiting attention by a non-existent sexton.

"All of us go down to the grave, yet even here we make our song alleluia...."

Mary was more than a committed Presbyterian

    desperately holding her local congregation together,

        defiant not only of decline of average Sunday attendance, but also the cancer which ravaged

    her body.

Something eternal burned within her,

    a passion for belonging.

        Mary's welcoming smile,

            and the ability to open her home and life to all people....

"Yet even at the grave we make our song: Alleluia, alleluia, alleluia."

    The refrains chase the cob-webs

        from the corners of the nave.

                November 29, 2012

Political Process Upside Down

No one had planned to take an offering,

    but generosity cannot be squelched.

        A few dollar bills thrown down by the baptismal font-a passerby picked them up trying

            to correct an accidental loss.

More followed.

    Congregants having to step over

        the growing spill of unplanned offering.

The accountants and treasurer anxious

    on how will it be counted, controlled and appropriately channeled.

        This is not best practice according to our manual of business affairs.

But the abundance of generosity floods over the floor,

    a mosaic of bills embarrassing the powers that planned an efficient liturgy, but failed to accommodate the capricious Spirit.

This is the way of God,

    to bubble up, underfoot, unplanned, to trip us up.

July 7, 2012

Long Leg

The long hallway from the staff parking lot to the
    elevator bank did not make the priority list

        for remodeling.

            It was utilitarian.

The below ground hallway was solely a means of moving
    staff, carts, flowers, deliveries and an occasional body
    to the Morgue.

        Guests (they used to be called patients)

            are not supposed to be down here.

The drab gray wall paper only went half way down,

    its conquest broken by the plastic rub rail to keep
    supply carts from damaging the walls.

        Less expensive gray paint covered dings

            collected over the years.

Occasionally, a silver convex mirror hung from a corner
    provides warning of a cart coming out of

        "Housekeeping" or "Durable Materials."

Does "Security" hide a camera behind the silver bulbous eye?

    Am I cynical in thinking it was put there

        to cut down accidents and cost of litigation?

I have walked this underground hallway many times,

    on my way to visit parishioners in the ICU.

A mental game of memorizing the order of the cheaply framed art prints some decorator used to soften

    the institutional feel.

        Van Gogh's "Starry Night" next to the locked Morgue….

        was the irony intentional?

        A Pissarro across from the material handling office.

At the turn next to the elevator is my favorite,

    Edward Hopper's, "The Long Leg."

Maybe it was the long horizontal line,

    broken only by the sailboat on starboard tack,

        the blue peaceful water inviting,

            recalling long tricks at the helm,

                not wanting to finish the day sail and

                      go back to the work and drudgery of home.

The gentle curve of jib against the gaff rigged mainsail

    gave me a moment's respite from thinking about what I was going to find awaiting in the ICU.

And so I return to the hard work ahead

    of reminding people that death is not the enemy

        and is a natural part of our journey.

I wonder if the workman who hung the various prints

    had any inkling of the poetic flair for this placement.

I wonder, do the surgeons, pastors and
    morticians contemplate the meaning as
    we wait

        for the ding of our elevator?

Or does art make the world into poetry?

                May 5, 2015

Waiting on Henri Ross

The fetal heart monitor fills the darkened room with those magical sounds.

    Whoosh, whoosh, whoosh….

        Not quite fluids going through a pump,

            nor is it like drums of a percussionist.

                It is a more ancient spiritual music.

I know the sound,

    not just from visiting other women who are in labor,

        but it is the sound which speaks to a deep place in my memory.

Rhythmic patterns with interruptions caused by your turning and jostling for room,

        bring a smile and glimmer of who is to come.

This music is much more effective than all the techniques of centering prayer,

        yoga or the other practices I have tried or taught….

But I can't linger to hear, to worship….

Your mother is resting, preparing.

The labor and delivery room is not my sacristy or altar,

so I leave to wait

amid the harsher sounds you will soon hear.

June 29, 2012

Lament

How can I be reconciled to the loss?

    We shared so much life.

        We kept vigil during your child's birth,

            baptized, drank coffee, shared dreams, fears and hopes.

A Ninja turtle piñata made me nervous

    as young Henri swung a bat in an expectant crowd.

        That is how we celebrated a birthday and promotions.

In gentleness and strength

    you would rock a restless child through the Prayers of the People.

        Ensconced on the Gospel side, you are a fixture on Sunday morning.

That distant Sunday when your oldest wanted to receive communion, two-year-old arms reached out for bread

with a binky in one hand….

> A youthful theological declaration of belonging and desire.

>> Recollections of holy moments in ministry.

And now you are moving. …to be near family.

A pastor's heart is always splintered.

> Pieces of me transfer to new towns and relocate.

> We promise to visit, to hold you in our prayers.

> But the loss is real.

>> Those chairs will always be vacant

>>> even if some new family sits where you used to pray.

When the deacon invites you to, "Go in peace to love and serve!"

> It has always been with the expectation of your returning.

Coming and going we can handle….

not leaving….

A tear falls as I break the bread to be shared,

I mask with a smile, and try to convince myself with an alleluia….

but for now,

I elevate a basket of fragments.

The gifts of God for the people of God.

January 6, 2016

Artifact

There are days when I realize

> we are all "interim" pastors.

>> I am privileged to preside from this altar for

>>> a short time, five, ten maybe even twenty-five years.

>>>> But very soon, I will be the old retired priest.

He told us to cast a net, to draw people and hold them in the Kingdom.

> And I have worked hard to do so and to make disciples.

>> My tenure could be measured in visits, cold calls, notes, invites to church, sermons preached,

>>> jail and hospital visits all over this county.

We add a family here; a lapsed member

> comes back, and as soon as we gather more into the parish family, someone dies,

or a business relocates to Dallas
taking with it an active family
with two kids.

Our Average Sunday
Attendance remains
the same.

The list of those whom I have buried grows year by year.

They aren't just names and services, but friends,

people with whom I have visited, prayed,

sat with while doctors gave test results.

I have heard their fears and sins

and shared in their hopes.

Changed by shared life and love.

But somehow that isn't measured on our annual
parochial report, and we clergy, like the rest of world,

serve the god of success and growth.

On those days when I am ready to move on,

I get out the old green leather bound parish register

in which we record all the sacraments.

The names of children baptized, adults confirmed, and marriages celebrated, going all the way back to the first book.

In the parish register in 1845,

on the bottom line where the priest in charge is to sign -Is his name….

Jackson Kemper.

The famous missionary whom I studied in seminary

and the church upholds in our calendar of saints.

I get a strange thrill that this well-known and respected saint, was once where I am now.

Did Jackson Kemper worry about closing the holes in the net?

How did a saint measure faithfulness?

He started so many schools, churches and even a seminary.

Was he filled with an abiding anxiety,

    a relentless need to grow the church?

        Would he begrudge my stewardship of what he started?

Today, I trace his name with my index finger,

    and touch the page where he wrote with a bold flourish.

An artifact, an outward and visible talisman.

    To touch the page, the lasting smudge of ink,

        blesses me with a sense of solidarity and strengthens me, so I can keep going

    for one more annual report.

                September 1, 2015

It is summer

It is summer when the smell of heated tar

    rises off the concrete parking lot

        and mixes with the smell of suntan lotion.

The lawn must be mowed before we can go to the swimming pool.

    The allergy-laden grass

        will stain my white socks and Converse tennis shoes a pale green.

In a few hours my skin will tingle from the sunburn

    and my eyes will be blurred from the chlorine.

        These are the halcyon days of summer, and what I remember most.

                May 29, 2014

Opening Day

On the Opening Day of the Season, nothing moves in
 the dry furnace heat except the thin weeds

    and brown stalks of sunflowers.

        Cicadas must be telling the doves

            that I am standing next to the telephone
            pole.

A metronome of summer sound arising along the fence
 row, the afternoon heat shimmers over the field.

A pair of dove land on the telephone wire a hundred
 yards off, undoubtedly warned to stay out of range.

    They linger and then fly towards the pond.

        Late afternoon is not time to be anywhere
        except in the shade.

The 20-gauge Browning over and under is warm,

    and so I hold it in the crook of my elbow,

        allowing the camouflage shirt to buffer….

Even the AA shells which I hold in the palm
of my hand reminds me that this dry time

of year is really our Lent.

The crops are gone, only remnants of grain

yet to be scavenged and devoured by field mice.

The doves are migrating; they too know of
changing seasons.

June 25, 2012

Late Summer Tomatoes

The cage and stakes I put in

    to imprison your spindly body was futile.

The weight of all the green tomatoes

    enabled your arms to escape the cage

        and you fled onto the neighboring holly.

Behind the prickly bush

    you are hiding a few ripe cherry tomatoes.

        The bright red contrasting with the straw brown of

            the vines and the light green of the holly.

I have to lean over cage and bush to gather you.

    You think camouflaged in the holly

        we will mistake you for the poisonous
        berries, but ha!

            I am militant and captain of my garden.

Protected by the bush and its prickly spiny leaves,

    I reach forth my hand to do combat.

With the slightest touch you fall off the vine

    and escape onto the ground.

Now, I have to act like the little plastic army men

    I used to play with as a child,

        and crawl on my hands and knees

            to reach underneath the bush….

                My knee finds a dry holly leaf

                      and gets stuck by the crisp pointed spine.

                      Ouch, a wounded soldier.

The scent of vines envelopes me as I lean,

    reach, and stretch to capture the fallen fruit.

That is the way of late summer,

   no grace-filled easy harvest,

     no leisurely picking with a basket.

        For tonight's salad

           you have to do recon and urban
           backyard bush combat.

                        July 23, 2012

Sunflower

How did you pop up in the mulch amidst the arranged pots and water feature?

> Your wild randomness upsetting the artful coreopsis and geraniums.
>
>> My hand paused as I grabbed your tough stem to dislodge you and throw you into the pile of mulch.

On a whim I left you alone, to see what might come....

You are much more subtle and complicated

> than your rough hairy neck portrays.
>
> The flowers in your head spiral
>
>> creating a pattern with mathematical precision which only a Fibonacci number can describe.

Like a child's face staring up at the morning sun,

> you reached with such vigor,
>
>> until heavy with seeds you bent over

looking at the ground.

Do sunflowers get osteoporosis?

I could understand how your head got so heavy

with thoughts so it was just too much to look up…

you were tired.. even the yellow rimming your face

began to turn dusty.

A grasshopper violating your leaves
munched a few holes.

A purple finch landed on your head causing a slight
sway, and then bent over and began

plucking out seeds.

First along the rim, closest to his feet which
gripped your scalp.

The once perfect spiral of seeds standing shoulder to
shoulder in geometric succession,

now broken to meet his hunger.

Each day more seeds are plucked out

a brown patch like a cancer spreads
across your once proud head.

He spoke of seeds in parables,

    falling on the beaten path, among thorns, and in good soil.

        Maybe the parable should have been extended

            to teach us about life, passion, and purpose.

                Theological insight on decay and death.

Maybe the lesson is the wild randomness of it all,

    how the pots and placed driftwood are not nearly as magnificent as the life of a sunflower seed

        scattered by a bird

           and left alone to see what might come.

                      June 19, 2012

Grandfather Spindler

The naval uniform dates from the Spanish American War.

    I know as little of that war as I do of you.

        Your photograph sits on the bookshelf,

            appropriately near all the volumes of sailing, Patrick O'Brien, and Nelson.

Infected by the patriotic fervor after the sinking of the Maine, as a young man you signed on

    to help liberate Cuba from the Spanish Empire.

        I wonder if you got to fight with the Rough Riders, or, like so many of your comrades,

            were you incapacitated by yellow fever?

What I do know is that you were the gentle grandfather

    who played checkers,

        ushered at the Methodist Church,

            and discreetly slipped Life Savers to your granddaughter.

                              June 27, 2012

Black Shoes

Cautiously she asked, "Did you get dressed in the dark?"

> It is a gift of simplicity that as a priest I only wear black,
>> never having to worry about mixing blue and black socks.

She smiled and pointed at my feet….

I was wearing two different shoes.

Both black loafers, one with a buckle and the other more plain.

> Seemed so obvious once she pointed them out with a slight giggle.
>> "Hope that fills your day with a little laughter."

After the initial surprise

> I tried to feel the difference between my left and right foot, scrunching my feet and curling
>> my toes under

to see if piggy gymnastics would reveal
tactile clues.

My brain couldn't register the
slight difference in heel
height or the

narrowness of toe cap.

I had gone all day without awareness of my slight faux pas.

I wonder how many people had noticed and been silent.

Before her giggle and loving smile

my appearance was low on my conscious radar.

But immediately, I felt myself back in Jr. High

not wanting to stick out and be different,

providing ammunition to those who would ridicule.

It is ironic that I would be comfortable walking around Wednesday with a smudge of ash on my forehead,

but to avoid more shame,

before my next appointment I would drive home and change.

I ponder, should I take off the left one

so the right could match,

or the right so the left would rejoin its twin?

Along the welt of the left one,

a light brown smear of mud.

Oklahoma red dirt ….would fail inspection by the Altar Guild.

Surely there was a preachable moment in this,

an insight into humanity and our need to be found acceptable.

A gift of what it means to be broken and redeemed.

Maybe it is the power of social shaping, or maybe

the dust was another reminder of the mortality

we can't avoid.

September 3, 2015

Bull Trout

The phone call came after we had gone to bed,

    the immediate panic of what's wrong was displaced

        as soon as I heard your voice.

Your words conveyed joy,

    not bragging really, just the joy of wanting to share….

"Dad, I wanted you to know I caught my largest 'Bullie' ever!"

    Not Bull Trout, but the familiar phrase

        used by guides and those "in the business."

"And the coolest thing," you said,

    "was that I caught it on a streamer that I had tied myself."

        You relived the fish hitting the fly,

            the fight and struggle with the net,

                and for a few minutes, I wasn't in my bed in Oklahoma

but with you on the Blackfoot
in Montana.

The photo you e-mailed

    shows your wide smile slightly above the dorsal fin.

You hold the fish to accentuate the length,

    an old guide's trick, pushing the head forward, arms outstretched, even with that, it is a beautiful fish.

        The pink spots on its belly

            showing the resemblance to the Dolly Varden we caught in Alaska,

                when you were first learning to cast a fly.

The white underbelly and marks on the leading edge of the pectoral fins,

    giving that distinctive flash when it turns

        and runs down river after you have set the hook.

Because I know you,

    that fish was released to be caught another day,

        but this call,

            this photo, will stand forever as a trophy,

                not for the size of fish,

                    but for the man you have become.

                                  June 21, 2012

Where did Summer Go?

I had all these plans, long leisurely days at the lake,

time away to read, and just laze around.

But the newspaper has "Back-to-School"
ads, and this morning,

a light fog, hovered over Haikey
Creek....

it was only 59 degrees.

This is not summer on the plains,

when the cicadas and dry heat lingers.

The blazing sun bakes the Johnson grass

till it rustles with a brittle rasping sound....

Summer's "death rattle"

which comes right before the end.

Soon a frost will wilt the Morning Glories hanging over
the fence and inevitably fall will be over....

But I didn't get to linger in the summer,

time pushed us out of my Eden

and we reluctantly trudge toward winter.

August 26, 2015

CA-35

I jog by while you are walking hand in hand

    down the urban canal.

        You show no concern or unease with the openness of your love.

I grew up in a time where we would have thrown stones or at least pointed and gawked.

        The shaded luxury apartments with overarching pergolas bear witness to the architectural

            sensitivity and wealth of this city.

Jogging around the canal cooled by fountains

    I wonder how this happened and who paid for this?

Stretching my calf muscles next to a granite marker

    I read about the dramatic sinking of the USS Indianapolis.

So many struggled in the water, burned by explosions, sharks feasting, exposure....

dying of thirst.

My question answered.

July 4, 2012

Release

Perhaps bicycles are a foretaste

>of what it will be like to be released from our bodies.

I didn't know it then,

>but as a child coasting on my Schwinn ten speed
>
>>after cresting the hill is as close to freedom as you can get.

Riding, I am higher than I would stand,

>and more swift than if I ran....
>
>>The rushing wind fills my ears until I turn.

The southern wind now pushing the back of my windbreaker propels me.

>The wind tumbles the cottonwood leaves
>
>>down the road.
>>
>>>Immediately, all becomes quiet.

Jolts caused by the joints in the concrete
slabs are transmitted to my arms

    and then up to my shoulders....

        my teeth jar every twenty feet.

At the intersection, a new section of blacktop,

    smooth and without blemish,

        the bike nearly silent.

I have made this run so often,

    I know at which point I can quit peddling

        and coast the two houses until my drive.

Arriving at home, I simply lay the bike on the grass,

    flying into the house, giving no more attention to
    the Schwinn than a dragonfly leaving its

        hardened nymph stage behind.

                February 26, 2013

Baccalaureate

Prelude in E Flat

Themes pass from hand to hand,

    rank to rank.

        Pedals kicking around the motif.

Grandparents sit with pride

    as young graduates perch uneasily in tie and high heels.

Wake up young grads!

    Listen! The theme is playing for you.

        It is your time to own the refrain

            and then add your own improvisations.

All of creation waits to hear your great opus.

                              June 6, 2012

Tiananmen Square

Standing still, head slightly bowed,

    vulnerable

        you hold a satchel (as my mom would call it)

        and a bag of groceries….

            ….you face four tanks, and they stop….

The grainy image tells us the photographer was safely far away when that shot was taken.

    I am not sure we ever knew your name,

        or if you were killed and your body

            disposed of during the crackdown.

You bear witness to courage,

    to something stronger than tanks, regimes and oppression.

It is hard to believe it has been a quarter of a century….

    Did you know you would inspire others,

and that your non-violent protest would haunt
my complacency?

June 4, 2014

Marlinspike

The knot at the clew of the genoa

    had hardened.

        Tension and years of use had solidified the fibers into an unbending mass.

            Seasons of sun with rain and spray

                had made the strands of the once-pliable double braid inflexible.

        The white with blue fleck pattern had faded

            and taken on a green hue

                where water and dust had collected and molded.

My fingers worked until they ached,

    the knot was unyielding.

        The fid thrust into the center, an attempt to focus the force.

A different side of the knot was poked,
jabbed, pried…

A few bright strands of nylon fiber poked through the
dingy cover which had been pricked by the fid.

The knot was frozen.

Defeated, the fid was closed and the serrated blade
unleashed.

Sawing quickly through stiff fibers

bright white and blue flecks of fresh line never
exposed to light, shown through as the line

was cut….

Even when cut,

the knot refused to give up its hardened memory

of the bend and loop of the clew….

Some hurts are like that….

Pulled tightly in the dark chambers of memory….

Even when we gently bring them out

and examine them in the searching light of
love, the pain and the salt from tears

spilt long ago have taken away
suppleness.

I don't have a clue as to what it will take to remove
these knots in my memory….

But if my genoa sheet has anything to teach, it
will be painful.

September 11, 2014

Poem Depression

Depression has a voracious appetite,

    devouring all but the essential energy.

The grey Shadow consumes.

    It sneaks into the bedroom in the morning,

        permeating the air.

            Happiness and vitality evaporate into the mist....

Never fully sated,

    depression nibbles the edges of everything beautiful.

        It mutes the brilliance of the morning sun,

            a fog covering the dawn....

Coffee.

    Coffee helps, the warm mug is grounding, real and solid in my hands.

Listening to Weber's *Pie Jesu*, the music no longer exalts or soars,

    reduced to a somber part of a Requiem….

But in time….

    In time, the grey shadows of the day slowly lift,

        and in the fullness of time,

            light will come, displacing and piercing the shadows.

October 30, 2014

Dental X-rays

The dental assistant opened my mouth

    to put in some large apparatus containing film to take x-rays.

        It was uncomfortable, and while dwelling on it,

            the discomfort crossed over into the level of pain.

                My cheeks stretched to hurting, gums pinched….

"Oh, I almost forgot. Don't want you to have any harmful effects from the radiation,"

    as she laid the heavy lead apron over my body

    covering my neck, shoulders and chest.

        The bright yellow and cheery flower pattern of the plastic covering

            was a façade for the massive impenetrability which it contained….

It pressed down …. the heaviness depressed my rib cage, just enough to make my breathing slightly more shallow.

I felt as if I had retreated into a shell, sought refuge under armor…

The weighted apron immobilized me in a way which was familiar and strangely comforting.

I no longer focused on the discomfort of my gums.

Body-memory told me I know this place of hiddenness,

this sought-out refuge of protection,

the familiar sinking into depression and the invisible weight which has armored me against the pain of life….

Though I have hidden behind a protective covering with a wreathed façade,

shame and events from my childhood have already done cellular damage…

October 14, 2014

November Tear

The cool wetness of the tear surprised me.

    Following the path of least resistance

        it flowed down creases,

            following valleys created by years of squints and frowns.

Slowly the tear transverses the swell of my cheek

    and picking up speed gained by gravity,

        gets lost in my graying beard.

The November wind caused its telltale trail to demand a response….

    Without thought,

        my hand wipes away the cold remnants.

As I walk to the door to open it for a new day, I wonder why….

                                      November 8, 2012

Night Terrors

I am haunted the first few hours this morning.

The dreams which commandeered my sleep were stressful.

> I think I know that the fears are not grounded in truth,
>> but still I wonder….

I sit with another cup of coffee

> hoping the mist and darkness will dissipate
>> so I can be free of the weight, anxiety and questions.

I call just to see how work is going for you….

What I really want… what I need to know….

> is that we are ok.

> Your voice gives me a little piece of solid ground,
>> enough for one foot.

June 13, 2012

Winter Wind

Wind sounds different in the winter.

I am not sure how, but the slapping of shingles,

    and whoosh around the windows is not the same in April.

        It is more than the lack of leaves in the trees….

            It is more than the cool air which carries sound waves with less resistance.

It is the emptiness of cold.

    The dark whisper warns me to bury myself under the covers, pull the pillow over my head and hide.

        This is the time for waiting, a time for hibernating,

            the solstice is still a week away….

                We have more darkness to brave.

                      December 17, 2014

The Grand Floridian Hotel

The Grand Floridian Hotel

>pipes in the smell of pralines to contrive the feel of a bygone era.

>>The housekeepers are referred to as "cast,"

>>>and the architecture is well thought out.

New building codes accommodate obese visitors in electric scooters to have their magical "experience."

>The lake is also manmade design of the Disney show.

Getting off the property and being able to go to a chain pharmacy which sells nicotine patches, Band-Aids,

>and condoms is not feasible….

Give me something real….earthy, not perfect.

>I want to see the wild randomness

>>of a flower growing in the crack of a parkinglot,

and a woman wearing a creased brow of worry,

rather than the plastic smile of a character.

December 1, 2014

Post-election

There are times when I don't feel like I belong.

    When traveling in a foreign county,

        at the ritzy yacht club,

            or at the VFW.

Not that I don't like the people there and find some things in common.

Life planted me here, and not there,

    in times of peace,

        and not when I would have been drafted.

            We are just different….

But this morning,

    I feel like I don't belong in my home state.

        The re-elected Governor has a proven track record of hurting education, and immigrants

and is opposed to expanding medical
insurance for women and children.

Yet she has overwhelmingly won the
vote.

I sigh, and wonder how my values and religious
convictions have made me so alien to the state

in which I was born and raised.

So I will ignore the victorious posts on social media,

and swallow bile when someone claims the
outcome as God's blessing.

Today, I will volunteer again at the feeding
program and wonder how long....

November 5, 2014

Old Truck

The old truck was painted brown and had mud caked on
its fender and bumper.

> A dog, three boys, and Dad all squeezed into the
> cab for an early morning duck hunt going
> out to the pond known as "Windmill,"

The pond named after the rusting steel skeleton

> which only held up two vanes,

>> the others missing, fallen into the empty
>> livestock tank at its base.

Even though I had two layers of clothes on,

> and hand-me-down hunting boots, I was freezing.

> Boomer was warm sitting next to me,

>> his nose occasionally touched the angled
>> windshield of the pickup,

>>> leaving a wet nose impression
>>> surrounded in steam.

As we pulled off the road onto the winding dirt road

> which would lead us to the stand of blackjack trees next to the pond dam, Boomer's tail began thumping wildly in

>> anticipation of the sound of flights of Scaup and

>>> Pintails and Dad saying, "Get-em boys!"

Though I wasn't tall enough to shoot that year,

> it was still fun to be with my brothers in the blind,

>> out on my first hunt.

A faithful hunting dog,

> hot chocolate in the blind,

>> the surprisingly loud whistle of a flight of Redheads are what I remember most.

Boomer died in '74, and we buried him near that pond.

> Hot chocolate gave way to coffee in college,

and Dad stopped hunting the season he got cancer.

I wonder where that old truck is now.

November 19, 2014

Canine Cologne

The look on your face as you roll in the dead carp reveals utter bliss.

You deftly smear some drying scales behind your floppy ear.

    You are so proud of yourself....

        It is a sensual, biological yearning

            which eludes me....

On the drive home from the lake

    I think of the tasks ahead- dog wash, shampoo,

        drying you off outside, and brushing out the sand burrs....

            you stick your head out the window,

                the bouquet of summer scents

                    making a big red letter day....

The next morning as I dash on a little aftershave,

    your nose twitches,

you watch bewildered...., why would we do
   such a thing?

                              June 18, 2012

Contentment

It would take months to learn

    that you were allowed to eat with the other dogs

        and to jump up on the bed.

            Your eyes had that uneasy, anxious look.

Perhaps it was more difficult than we could imagine,

    dumped by some family which couldn't afford you anymore.

        That Saturday we found you emaciated,
        following children and families,

            little did we know how you would
            change us, and that you would
            make our home complete....

Now you jump up confidently on the bed,

    allow your body to fall down in the shape of a parenthesis,

        resting your head on my chest as you stare in my eyes.

A few furtive moves of your eyebrows
and then a contented sigh.

You exhale and allow rest to enfold you.

June 11, 2012

Cocoon

I don't know why the word came to me in my dreams.

It is described by its composite letters.

The arms of the letter "C" wrap around forming a nice warm envelope.

A few of the letters in the noun are already completely formed,

sealing off the world and providing an isolated space

while something develops inside.

I guess I have always liked small spaces.

A pillow fort as a child, the tree house of my youth and now the V berth of the boat.

The walls enfold and create a small space.

I see the space not as a place of protection,

but more as a place set apart, a space of focus.

Within my cocoon, there is enough fulfillment.

In my fort, I was sufficient.

> The army men and blanket, perhaps a Mattel car or two.
>
>> High in the tree house, it was enough to have a BB gun, pocketknife and soda can.

These were not small spaces in which to hide and seek protection but the place in which to begin

> an adventure....

Maybe that is why we cuddle in the boat the way we do at night.

> My arms wrap around you forming an envelope,
>
>> a small space of sufficiency and focus.
>
>> Our own little covering in which our love matures and develops.

>>> November 13, 2014

Liminal

It is hard to discern where your body starts and mine ends.

    My leg is over your leg, our hands entwined,

        a foot plays with your heel,

            the back of my leg lays over your thigh….

The rhythmic gentle movements of your breasts as you breathe invites me to breathe at the same rate….

I am not sure if my body is holding you down

    or your body is holding me up….

        Sleep is not far off,

            neither is the heat and passion of making love, but for now we float,

        in between,

            lost to self, fully one.

                          June 26, 2012

Vesper Light

"Now as we come to the vesper light,

    we sing thy praises" From Compline

When the rush of the day is over

    and the fading daylight enters through the patio door,

        that is when our bedroom becomes a refuge.

Gazing through the slats in the door

    diffuse horizontal bands of vesper light illumine the edge of your breast.

        You search for the mockingbird as she sings from her roost.

        Her bedroom is the gnarled, ice broken Bradford Pear

            hanging over our fence.

Books on the nightstand await,

    our feet seek the familiar touch and entwine.

This is our compline,

and we are grateful.

June 10, 2015

Shower

It is a choreographed ballet

    synchronized by years of morning routine….

        The shower has its ritual

            and order of operations.

                Shampoo, conditioner, face wash, soap.

We change places under the warm shower, as you rinse….

    My hands rest on both sides of your hips.

        You close your eyes and tilt your head back

            to rinse the conditioner out of your hair.

The water cascading down your shoulders and over your breasts.

I want to slow the routine, and linger, allow my hands to caress….

but work calls, and as deftly as a curtain closes on a ballet, your left hand reaches for the faucet.

June 12, 2012

Samuel

I knew you were my son when you got up from your chair at the food court.

It wasn't revealed at the usual times of birth, watching you compete at a game,

> or when you walked triumphantly across the stage to receive a diploma.

No, it was much more subtle

and most likely not even noticed by anyone,

except me.

All six of us were crowded around a café table in the busy airport concourse,

heavy carry-on bags splayed around our feet.

> Tiredness and frustration arising from having to go through security and catch a delayed flight

made all of us a little edgy.

Your brother's expensive fly rod case fell from its precarious perch atop his backpack.

The case landed unnoticed behind his chair,

    where someone could have stepped on it.

He was already grumpy, and instead of alerting,

    you discreetly got up,

        returned it to a safe place

            and sat back down.

        A humble act, foreseeing and averting possible disaster,

            you protected and cared.

                A brother's love, a servant's heart revealed,

                    this father's joy.

                      Sint Maarten.

                      Princess Juliana Airport

Concerning this book...

This collection of poems reflects the author's search for the Divine in the cracks and crevices of life. While often overlooked, common life experiences host meaning and convey the transcendent. These short thought-provoking poems arise from daily experiences as a priest, sailor, husband and dog lover.

Concerning the photos...

The cover photo was taken by Craig Jackson at St. Patrick's Episcopal Church, Broken Arrow

Page 13 photo of main Street in Wagoner, Oklahoma was taken by the author.

Page 54 photo of Zach Scott taken by Stan Spoharski

Page 83 photo Old Truck taken by Tammie Maloney

Concerning the author...

Shelby H Scott served as a missionary in Central America, in Northern Indiana, and currently for more than twenty years as the Rector of Saint Patrick's Episcopal Church, in Broken Arrow, OK. He received his B.A. from Southwestern Oklahoma State University, and M.DIV., from Seabury Western in Evanston, IL. Shelby and his wife Becky together have four grown children, one grandchild, and three dogs. Sailing and cycling fill their free time and provide a nice balance to their vocations. Most of Shelby's fantasy life is filled with thoughts of "sailing away for a year and a day" on their boat Dulcinea.